A SACRIFICIAL ZINC

A SACRIFICIAL ZINC

MATTHEW COOPERMAN

Lena-Miles Wever Todd Poetry Series
PLEIADES PRESS
Warrensburg, Missouri
& Rock Hill, South Carolina

Published by Pleiades Press
Department of English & Philosophy
Central Missouri State University
Warrensburg, Missouri 64093
&
Department of English
Winthrop University
Rock Hill, SC 29733

Distributed by Louisiana State University Press

2 4 6 8 9 7 5 3 1
First Pleiades Press Printing, 2001

On the cover: *Outboard Motor*, Arthur Garfield Dove
William H. Lane Collection. ©2001 Museum of Fine Arts, Boston
Cover designed ©2001 by Joy Katz

Grateful acknowledgement is due to the following publications in which some of these poems, or versions thereof, originally appeared:
Chicago Review ("Marvell's Sun" as "The Walking Sun"); *Mid-American Review* ("World Said" as "What the World Said"); *Quarterly West* ("The Art of Navigation"); *Tampa Review* ("In Time," "Transience"); *Many Mountains Moving* ("Leaf or Tongue," "Success"); *The Journal* ("Geometry" as "Brushtroke and Wish"); *Denver Quarterly* ("Tongue Ruth," "History," "For Those Who Would Drown Him"); *Sycamore Review* ("What I've Called Elsewhere"); *Pavement Saw* ("Resembling Her"); *Sniper Logic* ("Further Aridity"); *Black Warrior Review* ("Waking or Sleeping"); *Connecticut Review* ("Them Apples," Section II of "California Dreaming" as "Tasting Green"); *Sonora Review* ("Field Trip"); *The Bellingham Review* ("s c a n s i o n"); *Colorado Review* ("Where You Are"); *Pleiades* ("shell-like," "Obituary"); *Fourteen Hills* ("Two Waters"); *Permafrost*: ("Russian Pictures," "Better if Used By"); *American Literary Review* ("E is for Evidence"); *New Orleans Review* ("A Mini-Mart Near Fresno," "My Brueghel"); *Controlled Burn* ("To a Child Arrived Too Soon"); *International Quarterly* ("Then Yetsirah"); *Quarter After Eight* ("Traveling Papers")

"Catering" and "BBQ Sauce," in "Then Yetsirah," originally appeared in quite different forms in *Kinesis* and *Cumberland Poetry Review* respectively.

A portion of this manuscript, entitled *Surge,* was published in chapbook form by The Kent State University Press. Thanks to Maggie Anderson, Alice Cone and Erin Holman for their assistance with that manuscript. Special thanks go out to Richard Deming, Janet Sylvester, Hoag Holmgren, Joy Katz and Kevin Prufer for their editorial heroics. Also, thanks to the Fine Arts Work Center in Provincetown, where many of these poems came into focus (a goodly lot you Fellows). A profound gratitude to all of my poetical teachers at Colgate, CU, and Ohio U. And finally, to Susan Ludvigson, thanks for caring and noticing.

For my parents, Sandy and Larry

CONTENTS

History

before the rain
the light

flutter of
a sun, a yawn

over the grass
shadow of a car, then

the car: History
has intention

Once there was...

begins to think *begun*
and then spools over

grasp too late, the grass
one step of light

travels, restless in the gesture
without moving
                    Slck Slck...
history has
dimension, entering
the next day

space, determined as any
map, perhaps

In a land far away...

stories tender
weight and mass, cities

spread out, in pools

the rain gathers
light the sky
                    or the car

A ship represents a complex assembly of structural components. It is, as a body soluble by seas, the whole as much as the symbol. In such a structure the behavior of any one component may lead to the failure of other components in a progressive manner. Civilized life leans in with its excess of books. Compelled by dependency, he searches for props. Of primary concern is corrosion. One definition of corrosion is to consume by slow degrees, and the business of many new technologies is to prevent the foul consumption of the ship's body.

Reckoning is the study of decay. In order to prevent corrosion, protection by sacrificial anodes presents the standard execution. These are eaten by the sea as a worm may enter the hull. A person is a worm and a hull. Citational. Such are the powers of transmission. The cathodic method is effected by mounting welded lugs to the hull in strategic locations. These anodes are made of zinc alloy (ZnAlCd), and shall hereafter by referred to as sacrificial zincs.

A Mini-Mart Near Fresno

"What peaches and what penumbras!"
—Allen Ginsberg

I was a child of love in a flowering town, canary yellows, a daisy chain,
        stunned particular of forgetting
            which was love,

which was just California stretched like an Indian drum between peace
        and Vietnam. Unrequited,

I was greenhoused sativa, the Wandering Jew, a kind of Walt walking
        divided streets, united, nostalgic in a placard maze.

I knew Sturm und Drang, Cheech and Chong, Wham-O, "Hell No,
        We Won't Go!"

The architecture of God was in the plan of the city: draft zone in the projects,
        Head Start in the parks, Southern Pacific regularity,
            divorce, quietude.

Let's say polling room, intricate busing I was, Black Panthers, blotter blue,
        ecumenical philosophy, a nuclear 2.2.

Such buzz and then such languor: how the marsh for the mall,
        the hill for the cross, the slough for the production
            of burning unguents.

How Warlocks, Alarm Clock, Symbionese Liberation…
        How probative sensibility, Question Authority, conjurations
            of chlorine and myrrh,

this family, country, beehive and molehill, what you can make of it, why.
        I loved the network of holiday boats, the shape of the hulls
            as they delivered the sea…

How eventuality, lull, level sands: whosoever wakes here eat these words:
        I was the Golden Hind of Camelot Arms, a little ecstasy, a little neon
            plaint: requite, requite, the lyric
                mercado I was.·

IN TIME

they will forget him. In distance they will make him speak. Still, rhythm is a kind of scalding that remains, little boy on a Big Wheel, the sound of the handbrake as it catches, the slide across magnolia leaves in the primary colors of fall. What enters and is refused. What begins in shrieks at twilight worked out in sex and work. Inheritance. Absolution. The patter of rain is a memory that nothing describes. The Buddhists say neither there nor not there and I enter at ease, write and erase. Sunshine begins the Chinese maple. Little boy picks up his plastic tricycle and watches the bruise on his elbow spread into some kind of sign. He wonders where his mother is, years from now who she is. Enters has a voice. As when rain burns the ground in another century, stops, begins again. In this way the theory of doors. Constellation. Contestation. Lao Tzu is poolside, dozing in Marin under a persimmon tree, the straps of a chaise lounge pinching his legs and back, the splash of happy bathers articulate, theirs and not there.

FIELD TRIP

Look out the window. There's a
          dead buffalo. And doesn't it just remind you
of summer time

               when you were in the wagon

and later at night you were lying
                    looking up
at the ceiling

          and the sky in your head
was not dissimilar to the landscape

and the guns went off
          smoking tourists   technicolor birds
and the prairie kept on burning.

               Who shot whom? Where
is the remote and why is it

               the landscape is moving
but the Ford is still?

There's a herd of elk next to
          the endtable chewing leaves

          and you think of yourself
as a hunter on the ceiling as

               Orion's quiver

driving arrows again
into mammoths   suburbs   stars

and later when you're just eating
          eggs   thoughts

of a pregnant couple go out
                    to the truck passing by
with its Mayflower moving

also riding waves
               and where is it that you're from?

blue planet, red star

perhaps to trace with a plea my town
I must tell you *luminaria*
golden mouths in party bags flickers
in the willows in the cribs
you would say sentimental
maybe right but in emblems
come over the blacktop like sunrise
solicit *trust   you can*
the star of man who wears it
mules then gears then die-cast toys
semaphores of a drying force to wax
the dawn this wine dark illusion
my social construction of
satellites acedia thirst I could add antennae
local color a general milkman
spiraling from rooftops like evolution
paradise would you hear me
in this cul de sac way
how a town assembles the promised She
stoplights Little Leagues who trust the stars
the Big Red Star of parking space
leafblowers the aerial view
a green vanishing what you'd call her hair
why once constellations maps on trees
rise up Titleist affliction in the Whispering Pines
this pasture enough for all
the joys and all the guns fables
that manifest destiny *wouldn't it be nice...*
and digital pet sounds my man
who wears the dream like merchandise
dreams a cave blenders a bear
I was kids playing nomad oil man Sioux
the middle of streets and lawns
unbridled mistress Land
like a game a self-polishing device
and trust to be able a flaming bag
luminaria allegories come across the doorstep
nicely you can if you believe a plea
my town pictured wrought with stars
the Big Red Star the thirsty star

TRANSIENCE

A jackhammer, a green leisure suit drying
near a white house, an elderly neighbor, mowing
happening somewhere the *bleet bleet* of trucks
as Travis Tritt twangs on the radio "oh darlin'"
and the phone rings, it rings Sunday Sunday
wherever you are, mid-morning static "this is NPR..."
all things considered it's the American drill

and the phone rings. It's a telemarketer—hello?—and she
tells me this is not about money. You see she's from
the Leukemia Foundation—do you know
about the Leukemia Foundation? "it's
the only medical organization in America whose sole purpose
is to develop cures for child and adult leukemia..."

I'm sympathetic I'm lonely and I listen
to her pitch which turns to magazines offered
"at a very substantial discount for a twelve month period
entirely of your own choosing" while I work
on the Times a poem an interview. I'm trying or will be
politely to conduct the day the interview which this
is curiously. Irony? Between lines the whole thing is oddly

yes Sunday, metacognition, alignment of planets and watches,
overly familiar endless projects I will finish today I will.
Time passes. Minute delays and switches pave the air.
Despite my confusion my voice is strong in the connection
something happens. Happiness, oh dialogic otherness!
except of course I don't want the magazines and so must
come up with a version of "no" which resembles the brush-off
of "moving..."

But I don't say that ("I didn't say that!") I tell her that I will
"in the near future be transient and so have no need
for the magazines." It's ventriloquisms, invention,
exchange of voices, roosts, perturbations the point of which
her tone changes she changes
as she wishes me an upturn in my events for the coming year.

It is a new year on the verge of the millennium and I
        appreciate it. We have spun a strange pact in the mowing gaps,
despite the most obvious intention we have and here the word
            transient burns my ear. Embarrassment, a slippage,
    a loss in flow moving on one place to another giving way
            to another...

    The assumption of course is I'm homeless or imminently
will be, and we *talk talk* on my telephone in my cozy apartment
    about my lack of a future phone. Stupendous! Why it's
the most effective brush-off ever delivered, goddammit
        Teri Gross it's true!
                        Where will I be when I need the magazines?
I feel so much voice in her voice a need for home, all of our Sundays
            strung together during this "now
    it's the Folk Hour..."

Dilation of iris, gather and swarm of the flock. Tail of a comet
    a minstrel, a kite. The Prairie Home I'm after yet again?
            It's love shack, fame hole, fleeting stare. I know
    I know? I'm vagrant to a place in the need for one
like June or Ruby or Patsy Cline, this passing quickly
    in and out of existence, such a brief stay or unwashed sojourn affecting
            results beyond itself, how the oscillation of a circuit
    because of a sudden change in load that is our natural state,
            embodied online happiness
        fugitive in its vanishing...

For Those Who Would Drown Him

Herman Melville, 1819-1891, possibly

the fingers that now guide the pen are but a passenger, a spectral hand that tremors tallow fields. The book of life is etchings by the seaside, some forest annotation wherefore channels past light through kelp, the devil's apron. A man is but a candle to ambition. His neck an industry to will, his violence something mounted to a stave. The ghost of space inhabits, turns out the domestic, turns the open boat into a corresponding coloring. The beast is Society. Strike through the mask. The whole Atlantic breaks here. We are crews unto ourselves

as Hart Crane, 1899-1932, these

are bewildering times, a baptism of fire or a fix in hell, the nail, griddle, and bowl of which a myth is bare essentials. Gratings and balconies with plenty of nodding whores, torrents of uniforms, tropics of lush machines. I am a feverish embryo hugely unforgiven, evidence of experience, fiddles into dissent. To love a man and see the blood rose of a fist is anything but the sea from which I sing. I will survive to write you

Charles Olson, 1910-1970. The natural body, America

is Space, a veil and swaddle. A net on this gray day I walk from Brown's Shoal to Bridger's Fort. Let there be born a new Banquet (or let me be gay in bed with some wild dame). The map of the body is Sisyphus. I push my rock across hills as sere as gold. Our human moment an Instrument, irreducible tremblings of thing and cod story. When I hear the petty practitioners attempt to disperse by spreading, like manure, pale emotions, Humanism, all summaries and consolidations, I am lost, a man at sea, a coffin from my country. Leave the roots on, O Melanctha! My heave to plumb a City and a past. Raise me up, a charge

: this span out your span. Whose story's not antiphonal? By small degrees this now and know is local, brazen dark. I swim and swim at the Y until I'm tired. Pods open. Street cleaners start earlier everyday. Almost automated (please help me across), I climb up into the millennial remains, continue birding.

Marvell's Sun

My friends, on foot, have circled
       the globe. Around the world together
in an embrace, "a surcingle pair
       to stitch two hemispheres…"

I like that, the sound, and their roving.
       I go to all the slide shows
with my side dish of garlic potatoes.
       Everyone smiles and drinks

the wine that has come up from the cellar,
       pressed, stamped, and bottled
en famille, clean feet or so we trust
       as we sip a Nouveau Beaujolais,

and watch the clouds of Nepal swirl
       across the screen, prayer
walls and flags of parti-colored dreams
       that keep coming true each harvest.

You see, they are pilgrims, and find a place
       each year they have never been,
and live there, amongst storms and yokes
       of leather-bound oxen, finding

themselves, an answer to their wandering,
       or arts at least, a *dorje* to lead them on.
My friends, on skis, ahead thirty yards
       in the snow, have asked me to this ridge

to light the Chinese New Year in a smudge
       of sage held up in the chapping wind.
A fire burned once every twelve years,
       "it will be beautiful," they say.

I notice that the sun is almost setting,
       a *deus ex machina*, I think, down
to warm our lives and help the crops. But no,
       that's much too bloated, a curse

of wishing Greek. The sun is rarely beautiful,
        not a god or burning sage. Just setting
like a sun, a coyless flash of hydrogen
        devoured in its time.

FURTHER ARIDITY

—for Ed Dorn

Geodes, key chains, bits of beadwork
and bone, Western Stock Show of
rawhide, white hats, limitless sky,

this iconography of absolutes, purple
mountain largeness and sand. Take
a minute to examine the cost,
the truck stop matinee, where Hank

and Smells-like-Tar sing *where*
oh where can he be? Pard'ner, a neon arm
is departure, Sunoco and aggregate

by the edge of wander. Put a coin
in the cow's mouth, get a Taco
Burger, *you just have to dig for wood*
and water. There are wishes

in progress, that doctrine made Him
Me, a pronoun for destiny, alkali springs,
bad blood. They call it convergence,

hard work, burning bush in the road.
Rumor has others placed in the general
store. It's Acme, Coyote
when the smoke hole clears.

Then spin Wheel 'o Fortune, bang
the Dutch oven again, it's painful
dinner time at Rusty Ducats. Listen—

through the gap we knife
when we remember, conquest
shifts in the waves of the salt plain:
a vision, saguaro, some gum. The same

footprints left for a hundred years
make good roadside attractions
minerals are. Little green

grass out here under a wash
of autos, oil wells. Black gold. Texas
up and down. Some boom or bust
like rest: biblical injunctions

against sleeping with another man's wife,
sleeping too often in the Red Desert Motel.
Why it's potash I'm inhaling when we are

what dust's insisting: one place, two tribes,
what has paved the way, so to speak,
of Airstream trailers, convex reflections
huge of California, sells

the settle back. *Oh Continental!*
skeletal remains, the trace of hope
on billboards, pale rider doing 80,

I-80, and the swish of rig tires
shipping historical sleep. Frontier decisions
glint parallel rails. The journey lies
between sage and sentimental, a land

that doesn't close. It's high lonesome, the ditty's
a toll booth, a sideling away
and Las Vegas in just one direction,

one way this line becomes roadmaps, *I'm in,*
are you listening? *fold,* because noisy
giftshops *pass,* and remember
The Brave People?

WHERE YOU ARE

is a mystery, face
at the corner of East and West, the pocked stare
of a dinner clown, eyes of suddenly
speech. Highways. Horizons. What was

said. Passing trees seem
a branch of familiar, brake of black pine
that says *know me*, says *how
could you be anywhere else?*

In the enormous face of the moon
dragged over the motel couch
family is a room you almost
live in. Dust motes in the drapes, the cabled

dish of night. That far away
and bend so close. He said *rest,
boy parallax, the haunting
of a house.* I remember

a creek filled with sumac, pungent
smell of mud and rot, a yard filled
with going nowhere, with going
and coming home. Water stands,

the bank to the creek holds up its vines,
a boy becomes wicked and lovely. Now speech
falls out of the sky
like a dinner bell. What was

is mystery. It rings. The wind turns,
where you are and again
my darkness double. He says *I am a wheel,
I am still a wheel…*

Continent, city, country, society:
the choice is never wide and never free.
And here, or there... No. Should we have stayed at
home, wherever that may be?

—Elizabeth Bishop

shell-like

starts with pale circumference a child's wrist
against beach towel cord grass stippled sky alternations
of currents that tick in the wrist again
he climbs down the bleached stairs to the fishing docks
lines of seine drying in salty squares the deck ropes curled
like snail shells braids on the head of a vaguely
German girl in school he will get here how
looking back will he see the ripe swirl
of her waist going round and round little death
in the tick of the rusty swing on the bluff
the talk in back seats burrow and crush of
hulls riding fenders weathers desires alternations say
ebb and flood in his hands going soft in the bucket
of mullet and sand dab and the skin
pearled as fish flesh a child's face returning
to its dark ground he will wake to
the fleet coming in from its catch in a net
cities blinking people working and eating the hours
switch on full of smoke and horns a barge
in the river a cold breeze blowing his towel
wrapped shell-like beginnings of drift
the glittering palm of the sea a pale circumference

OBITUARY

Tiny Tim, a.k.a. Herbert Khaury, died Saturday while singing his trademark song "Tip-Toe Thru the Tulips" at the International Ukulele Festival in Minneapolis. He was a diabetic. Had congestive heart disease too. But he sang in those absurd American flag pants and he meant it. *I remember carnations, white and red, a setting for cannons at school.* "Death is never polite," he crooned in between bites of egg salad. *It was firedrills, Veteran's Day, meeting the Officer, Priest.* Only in America could such a guy be a star. I loved him as a kid, his fey freedom. *What does the lyric say? Sweet land of liberty?* I watched him strum his ukulele on Carson as the furnace rumbled and ticked and my parents settled in under the crazy quilt. Once at a McGovern rally, catching him on TV singing his old sweet song. *Leafletting through the azaleas, the politics of belief, death is a doorbell, is never polite.* My father, who had had a few beers, started singing with him in that strained falsetto warble. *Tip-Toe Thru the Tulips.* Those fat hands strumming, *'tis of thee I sing.* Then my own hands strumming. *Let freedom ring.* Then dancing, dancing, *across vistas or youth, the shining sea,* the Redwood High Patriots' gym floor.

THEM APPLES

Vocables, husks
in my grandfather's pockets

coral lips, one in each sleeve

the man split
between seed and death's
dried leaf.

[MacKintosh, MacAdams, catch of one's eye]
He knew

the terrain of flagging trees

orchards strung in rain
after, lands a gash
return in heather.

[*Appel,* Dutch, appellation, name. *Pyrus malus,* symbol of fruitfulness,
pome, a charm for lovers.]

Wind blows a sweetness
across the plains

a child burns
in the still closet air.

[King David, Jonathan, Roxbury Russet. Taste of the forbidden.
Pippin

a woman in green.]

He knew the red finger
of rivers

["the relation of these betwixt our apple hoards"]

knife
to the neck of the vanishing
woods, words

ripe phoenix fruit.

California Dreaming

I.

Tunnels of noon   a lattice
sky overgrown   the prick

and thrill of blackberry
spilling its blood

your blood and the compact
space it required

tasting green   For the first
time in the thicket is

then the rest   dye's echo
All this for a course

in water's toil   its wend
to the bay

in the warm bed
of the creek
                    Replete

if snow
could fill this world

it would bleed
a dusty bloom

                    who

pollen on the leaves
shivered skin

24

II.

Peppered grains of asphalt
slide between the wheels

silver spokes glinting
their turn of sun

a long way from home
the swish of Malibus

powder-blue Impalas
all the way to the crotch

and shimmer of the bay

The center strip of the avenue
sheds a poisonous fume

pink and white flashing
all chrome

green oleander
                    wagging
a coastal wind

        El Camino Real, 1976

We're courting the Whopper
of San Antone

of hunger is something
a Spanglish tune

Our Way to the mall
a million servings

there are miles
between us

the labor of wharves

III.

    cluster of bees

        a Tab can   grass

a gold hum

    in the chest

        where eucalyptus

     sheds its silver

  and bark

     turns to smoke

in the summer sun

      a gold ball of resin

    to be caught between

dream   this

    and the chalky cliffs

WAKING OR SLEEPING

You sleep to feel the weight: ten thousand pounds
of ivy under the trees, olive greens, susurrations
of vein and bind inside the eyes.

That Steller's jay now caught in the mouth
of the oak is a type of sleep. A type of drink,
to see and scream on pyracantha wine

a neighbor listening. The braille of asphalt
remembers. It cracks. It reads you back, each step.
It reads the feel of feet like so much skin, routine.

Like so much sun. Gasoline, geranium, semen, mint.
In the white arms of laundry you smell nobody
home. Sleep to touch the body already gone.

HERMENEUTICA

1 String theory, pollywogs, spells of vanquished Ortho balms
 which fade in brown glass jugs. Efforts at Pi. Home movies

1.1 extolling The Final Day. Tiny ivory elephants. Kachina dolls
 like Matchbox cars, conflation and collecting. Oh cultures,

1.2 equilibration. "A Mason ring here is a Mason ring there."
 Ozone depletion and the question of where. Handshakes (three

2 fingers) I recall introducing the Way of the Shriner. Evolution's
 tiny hammer, say periodic tide, then table. The Bay of Fundi

2.2 my "so dramatic," four trawlers lying sideways in black mud,
 signaling. Simulacrum, mother's milk. Audubon's Baudrillard

3 and hills like white sentences. A primary criticism. A secondary
 panopticon. Care for the seat of the soul. Perhaps virago, index

4 of albedo, population growth, drag coefficiency. Faith. Amiens.
 Oral Roberts. Amen! "It's the perfect preparation of roasted meats,"

4.1 healthy and spit-basted by an astrologer who's also a trademark.
 It's the kestrel dying on the weathervane, my first house marked

4.2 by a paternal separation, the whir of the blender, hopeful ahs
 of Sunday dinner. It's Mach 1—boom!—three dabs of wasabi, something

5 something's heaven's gate, projection/reception through the stars
 of the Dumbbell Nebula. Black feelings. Confusion. Flamenco

5.1 dancers which give my duende voice. "The old laws of recurrence do
 wobble on the golden bough." Consiliance. A butterfly's wing

6 and cribbage, reading *The Andromeda Strain* by the yellow light
 of the hurricane. The screen goes blank, reconsiders, returns

7 with script in its hair. Hear "recourse to numerology, aliens, RAM."
 How interpretive strategies render X. The Nazdaqpeptide

7.1   Apocolypse Y. "Emptiness…" the monks begin chanting as glaciers calve into rise. "More the better!," I recalls, and "This one's Aramaic

8   for you my friend." Praise Gaia! Feng Shui! So late in your bathing suit, scrotum cold, "when She would say She did come?"

BETTER IF USED BY

"Sugar I like, yet I have no desire
To become sugar."
                    —Ram Prasad

Cas Eliot smokes a joint with my mother near the cheese plate. As introductions go, there's a limit to what can be done with freedom. Like press in the brain from last night's wine, or lull in the tongue from slack listening all these years. I was given a set of choices. A whole set. And I laid them down in the park to make a network of bird nest, eros, airplane glue. Emotionally, already I was indulgent and forgot things. The point, or the pool pump silence. Dinner hour, idealism, sleepy astringencies of the hundred year rosemary hedge. Sometimes the senses are anything but helpful. Like the White Rabbit that nibbled on my ear. Choices, arboreal, consumptive. The playpen of poisonous sweet flag that flourished then in the pipe. Now Hip Hop kidz wheel like sufis outside my window. Fly. They gave me the time and what for. Falling down is a habit, must be put to use.

Russian Pictures

Suppose a door out a window on the way to Minsk is a guardhouse and the border, gated zone in green flannel, kalashnikovs, red epaulets, and my father with his stealth Ricoh snapping conspiracies under his raincoat. Suppose the games of middle-aged men, of old men rheumy and dank. Of checkers, yes, the stench of cabbage, and my Jewish ghost walking the streets. Suppose it like exposure, emulsion's dying silver. I sit as still as a samovar and the black gate passes over me.

Sleeping alone, or so it seemed. Then babushkas menacing the dark. Bed check. A flashlight flying up like a struck match from a flour sack dress. The gripped click of the ViewMaster. A fever sweat under rough sheets. I'm eight on the 11th floor of the Sovietskya Hotel. I'm St. Basil's bells, how they peal: night from the neon rose of Stolichnya, a sickle of moon from a flag onto a sky.

Lost in the galleries of the Hermitage. Endless corridors of gleaming Icons, the scruff of heavy shoes. A bored Christ, rachitic. I tried to count faces, the occurrence of wounds. Each gaze held the invisible. The frame. The camera's eye. Whose eye? The ceiling's peeling wafer.

Here my Mother bears the strain: a daughter's cool sufficiency, a son's strange Slavic fear, a husband's need to place the vague romance of his name. Sprung, as if from her own foreignness, she battles bread queues, broken heels, workers hunkered around tea machines. A fierce wind off the Neva whips her paisley scarf into a threat. Review. The pastel crenellations of another city block, each frieze the face of Catherine. Advance. She stares them down, pushes with her net bag through the crowd.

Perhaps dancing quadrilles at the Summer Palace. The Czar's white trim of roses and black hearts. Click. Or the horse fountain galloping through a cloud of startled midges. A boy in wet Hush Puppies humming a song from America. "I've been through the desert on a horse with no name... it feels good to be out in the rain." And the beautiful grid of the city. And the shimmering banner of Breshnev. Carousel. By paternal miens. His red sash announcing announcing... click.

scansion

There is something suspicious in the line. And when
        you return there are floodlamps
around the stanza. A room. The idea
                of home, the bright cathedral of childhood
a convenience store at the end of Whipple St. (When

did I leave? When did I do the last thing last?)

You go fishing, loving the old cast. The lake at camp,
        the coffee can wormy and black, the rickety dock
you knew would last forever. And it did, in that
        moment, that room. You go back. You are still and you are

moving, across the page, down the road, making time
        for the coast. It's a photo of four resembling clamor,
sno cones, water wings, windy Junes. (Here

notice the stretch in a poem about matter, stresses and meters.
                A catalog.
        Heartbeat. Duple foot. Shell game
that is moveable, the way myth or pledges endure.)

                But the line ends, rewinds, does not hold the rhyme
to the end of the song. We start out one place, end up

planting marigolds in a rented house to keep the enormous snails out.
        Things to leave traces: the silver fluorescence
                of each light; a fly cast into the lake's
eye, circles widening into verbs and intentions
        that wish the sign into memory. To blossom

back, fix and throw. *Arrow.* A vulgar corruption. *Ev'r. Every.*
        To survey the bow and twinge. There is
something suspicious in verse, in the way a word
        returns. *I* leaves, grows
children, calls from a neighboring state. *You* remain, are
        still. (Moving takes

a time and takes another.) Words are a sign for surface,
                a form of home that doesn't scan.
Another room. Where are you? Subject. Substance. Seem. These feet
        are merely consignment, a light at the end of the block,
a twenty-four hour convenience store, idylls
                        where you get in line.

WHAT I'VE CALLED ELSEWHERE

"The ways we miss our lives are life."
—Randall Jarrell

1

A reclining chair in childhood. A sag
where father sat, pressures of his dark
forearms oiling the intricate weave, young
eyes glistening to the radio's slow geometry.

A rapture shaped like wings, like imagining
fathers flying over emerald lawns. He sings
            the evening paper into air.

2

On a phonograph in Montmartre Ella cries
for what is lost, and a naked woman
strokes the morning light, her cigarette and sighs
curling towards the open window. Sad scene

she crosses like Degas' black mistress, waiting
for the sun to strike seven across her skin.
The wallpaper sighs, warms to Prussian blue.
On the street, *Ain't Misbehavin'* and *poisson frais.*

3

Pause. To revise. Gather. A jet seaming sky somewhere
over Wisconsin. A family shifting patio furniture
into dusk in California. Destinies so manifest, facts:

romas from the garden glisten in olive oil
as orange dragonflies weave the fading sun into the skin

4

of a pool. What surfaces shine between states and rooms?

5

It is the local storm. As far as I can see it's iron ocean,
waves reckless cresting over the bow, *one, two,* and snow,
       snow, falling thick as fog. It is

a car wreck, surgery, a lover's scent. A long time
since then, and where it was, stilled dime of a porch light
       which falls precisely here

6

and here: high harvest. Bales of wheat in ocher fields,
years of faith in ancient means
as we are elsewhere, a young mother hurtling
down a summer road, her bare shoulders caught
       in the passing glass truck.

7

Rest stops, jokes, moans in rented rooms. Times
the elegant abacus subtracts, journeying town to town,
       the voice of the one I miss linking searching

to surface. *We are the lost light of what's said,* you say,
taking another drag. *Like the tick of all wandering*
       the moon sweeps over you sweeps over me

8

to a gathering, fading facts: our numbers count, who is and is not
there. And how to make up for the delay of not finding what?

9

in Rome, years ago. A photographer leans on the blackened
railing of the Saint Angelo. Humming. Dark forearms.
He counts Our Fathers as terns dip the Tiber. Church bells toll:
vespers, shining coins. There is soot gathering in the folds
       of his sleeves, calico on his hands, how

10

the moon is your question and answer, you say, *the moon
on water from the dock.* The broken silver, and your arms,
       every hair, sparked before the sudden water.

Every life is many days, day after day. We walk through ourselves, meeting robbers, ghosts, giants, old men, young men, wives, widows, brothers in love. But always meeting ourselves. The playwright who wrote the folio of this world.... is doubtless all in all in all of us, ostler and butcher, and would be bawd and cuckold too, but that in the economy of heaven, foretold by Hamlet, there are no more marriages, glorified man, an androgynous angel, being a wife unto himself.

—James Joyce

TWO WATERS

Body-surfing the break at Bean Hollow,
   the blue Pacific exactly the color of cold,
      I hold to the wave and am swept through a
         forest of kelp. The slippery bulbs parting,
           the rocks and shells parting, the various lights
             of the harbor. How the sea seems to set
               and not set, and the sleepy ground fog of late-
                  summer wintering into me, neither vaporous
                  nor inexact. Dusk drives on. Highway 1
                sparkles like white and red jewels on the nape
             of a woman I once knew. *Once* and *knew,*
           successions of cities, frame and body.
         Making love in an Upper West Side apart-
       ment. A row of Chandon White Star bottles
     shimmering in candlelight. Expense and then
   some distance. *A woman I once knew.*
 Incarnations, families, vessels of record, what
makes up the song, what fills up the time?

           My father loved sailing but not the beach,
           it was waves and it was not dunes.
               Filial flaw, I have
           his ankles, bony like egrets, step
           into the mud, feel the cool suck down,

           down, in the sedge, salt crusting black mud,
           north wind gusting in pampas grass, the click-
                  ing pod-weed husks.

   love is locations   names
         of the stains

            mother   father

  lover
      wind

                    song which is
        a gathering man's

                                where? and scattering
                    bone by bone

            what?

                                in his bag
        in his suit of skin

   Clam shells, gulls, tar and yellow seafoam. Six-pack rings, pitted styro-
foam, cobbles and driftwood snares. In grade school we would come to the
coast on field trips. Drake's Bay. Traveling songs. Biology. The bright bus
rolling through fog, the damp gray destination never the beach on TV.
   In third grade I found a dying seal at the little delta of San Gregorio
Creek. Its sad salt-spangled eyes, waiting. The distant cry of classmate's
screams lost in a wind-water sound. Everything humming as I watched. As
we watched, and waited.

        To draw a bird in the sand,
        to find a way to the word
        which resembles the shore
        mumbling forward, thumbing
        back, the grip of beginning
        an old love that's silver and torn.

        Something replaces the past
        (lover, nostalgia, resistance).
        Like the next wave you notice
        the next wave, how knowing's
        a wake, a hand in the ocean,
        counting the semblances,
        sounding the water's return.

The Ohlone called it *sa'ka nepu*: waters to be eaten, home. So much fish and game. A feasting tied to tides. To the falling acorn, the silver run of salmon. When the Spanish fathers came the Ohlone were amazed and confused. They called the padres Children of the Mules. With their glass beads, clocks and shining crosses the Ohlone believed them a new sort of God.

story is

school songs   history books

abalone ashtrays

Mission Days

wind in the bleachers that snuffs the tongue
where? string to a kite

her

ceaseless trail of

when?

My mother was always truthful. Not that she didn't lie but that she taught me where to tell the truth. In other words conviction, knowing what you believe in and when to say it. Vaguely Presbyterian, she converted to Judaism when she was eighteen. The belief in Justice, family. The knack for drama and song at each year's Seder.

Song. *When is it the cause of conviction? Can the voice be represented if the speaker is not?* God is a song for presences. The missing we do ourselves.

When my parents divorced it was "how we are, and how we are not." Locations in a series which marked out drift. Succession. Affair. Father flaw. Something in a body which is a cause. "Till death do us part" a song between lungs.

Between names: The Coop. My nickname in college. My father's. His father, suturing on the Main Line, learning the dark rules of American Jewry. An Ellis Island story. Alien, alias. The brand of a name that is not yours. Or to tell the truth and know it is only yours. "I am the land between saying and feeling." Marriage vow. That I will not. Feel. Betray. Extol. Corrupt. Voice is a name for beginning.   Begin—

because inside the moon is all symbol

because outside a shine a fulgent egg

because history
                    is fragments

I

in the sky
                                        what comes back
                and bleeds

teller's jagged tracery
                            shells   seeds   lies

what fills up the time?

    The noon bell rings over Ms. Jasper's instructions. She protests the explosive exit of her class, but what can she do? I sprint out of the room, slip at the top of the stairs and fall onto the small of my back. Out of air, I watch kids race out for Friday tacos. Chris Lafleur, her slow burn of cigarettes and wine. Steve Heffries, who will die in a car crash unceremoniously at eighteen. Billy Battie, married to Sharon Good and his father's Big Bill car dealership. Annette Warren, who I will finger in the balcony of the Laurel Theater during the climactic dance contest in *Saturday Night Fever*. In the airless pause of a fourth-grade noon I swim in Ms. Jasper's arms. The pale green walls. Everything slows

                and clouds

                    and breathes.

                                        A frame

                to a movie

successions of cities, a particular explanation of gender. What's to be known in the wake of beginnings? The missing we do ourselves. The problem of singing the present is deciding when it began.

For instance this skin, this literal frame. I remember my first "R" movie. *Vanishing Point,* an homage to '70s hippie excess. Blue language and the blue veil of tire smoke burning in the Mojave desert. Jujubees. Crushed velvet. A rumbling Barracuda. A naked woman rides a motorcycle in twilight. In and out of the dust and barrel cactus. Her rosy nipples bouncing, bouncing…

and then:

"…Aye, aye, aye, oh Lydia," my father singing to my embarrassment,
to my relatives at Thanksgiving, to the full moon shining through
the skylight when the first lie of my sex began to bloom.

She is lying on the waterbed, a dark reef of sin, of Styx,
"Come Sail Away," my first seductive song.

She is bleeding and wanting and I am bleeding and wanting.

and then:

What will we do in the morning? *The same as we do at night, my sweet. Turn off the something, turn on another.* She was tender and jagged in her New York apartment. Corn-pone portraits all teeth underneath. An artist's roar. The champagne and lingerie and linger. We ordered Chinese, addiction, stayed in for the lyrical moment.

The Ohlone called it hunger, *sa'ka nepu,* waters
of return, words to be ground, to stand on.
When a boy reached maturity he
was set out in a tule boat.
Seven days in a reed cup.
The waves rushing under
him, the rocking
sounds…

gambrel oak   bunch grass   indian paintbrush

     timothy   madrone   cormorant egg

Drake's Bay

        China White

           Upper West Side

Corruption's a part of the architecture.
I pick up the weave, the seething rhythm,
feel it in my soggy feet (memory's sieve
that drags the wake), walking in spring
with Mother off the Limantour dunes.

Nineteen years since we traced this stretch,
a film of sand candles, elastic pants
rolled to my knees, the swarming smoke
of sand flies curling in the updraft of waves.
What's in a song that's silver and torn?

semblances   orders   of once and knew

     of love is a father who pimps his daughter   bags
                  of blow
    in her bra

the shadow of everything too fast and slow

          cabs and cocks   the city
           inside her
   home

     in a word breaking down form

veins seeds scores drones

   wormwood   mescaria   Chinese poppy

On a recent trip to California I helped my mother buy a stereo for her new house. In generosity or pique she had given the old hi fi, which my father had bought, to the Catholic Worker's House. We went to a number of stores and finally found exactly the size and sound and price of what she wanted. We set it up on her new bookshelves. The house, all blond wood and windows, shimmered above the bay. The sound of Nina Simone rising and falling. *Do what you gotta do.* We drank some wine on the deck and watched the moon rise out of the redwood trees. It reminded me of a time sitting by the pool at the old house. The eerie scrim of water. The moon lolling in the tops of the white oaks. We had drunk numerous bottles of wine, and she told me that she had been married once before. How it didn't last more than a month. That her parents were mortified, scared, their independent daughter losing her way in the big city that was Milwaukee. That I was mortified, scared, an arbitrary son. *Do what you gotta do.* What did I know of this woman? A stranger passing through. That I wanted to. We threw acorns into the pool to break the stillness.

Story of the dark

Love problems, subjecthood, this is all our songs. In my movie I am whoring and painful. The credits reveal no rest. A sequel, as is a son, a pattern
     is only a pattern is only a pattern.

Sung (in theory)

    distance is not a safety net but a zone of tension

   my daily form a willing flame

      novel

  that we survive

that we cannot help but tell

        traveling in waves   restless traveling in see

           and seem   story is

     an I

      a mast

          at most and least

                  what   ·

   might have been

Sad bag of skin, how can we call this Justice? Love is a kite that keeps on raveling. Families of salt, dwindle, and rift. The missing we do ourselves.

Mother. Father. Lover. Other. The noon bell rings. I remember the times. Seen clearly. Felt. Despised and coveted. A truth at a distance. A particular explanation of gender.

No—

Love is this bottle of steak sauce, a barbecue day, my eyes on your crotch, a cold sweat breaking us down. Love is my body that crashes. The city gone to seed. One more day to say and feel, my arm a map, this vein oasis…

Stated, simply

that telling the truth gets you there. That words might but I cannot. Intentions gutter endlessly, and all this restless casting casting the sad metaphysic of sons.

Drake's Way, to break the nest.

My father sailed here, silent,
would wave offshore as he caught
the northerly out through the breakers.
Beat up past these Dover'd cliffs
to moor in Half Moon Bay.

Mirrored in surf, he holds
the lithe hand of his new wife
and dreams of his children
running this cusp of home.

I dream of a woman who resembles a city,
asleep, at rest, relieved, returned...
Autumn turns. A winter wind
begins the wide inscription.

Ohlone singing

"He has prepared himself since his father died. He has prepared himself.
All of you women get the pine needles, get the pines. He is going to do
the same as his father did. He has prepared himself since his father died..."

bodysong

thirty years
by the sea one
body to climb
back into yours
mine yours mine
one body

Paddling out through the stems of the
    bay, the big surf a translucent screen.
        The ocean turns to coinage in my hands.
        Silver *this* and silver *that,* image a
          love effervescent in each dip, *once*
           and *knew* in each stroke. God is this thrum
          of presentness. The missing we do ourselves.

Story of fear—

    So what is this blue light before me? A
    road to the shore that disappears, a boat,
    this moon, that body, shining through the skin
    of a poem? There are two waters in every
    life, one we have left, the other the gulf
    between waters. What I need are durations
    that compass the heart (season, forgiveness,
    alterity, sex), how to find a way to say loss
    that isn't, to find that I've always been
    home. Know is a word that embodies all
    at once. Word is an axis and becomes
    its own song (story, incarnation, lover, frame),
    that every family's a wave, and the blue
        Pacific exactly the color of cold.

Mother keeps digging for cherrystones in
spongy pickleweed. Late sun, shoulders
square to the sedge, she thrusts the shovel
into the open mouth of the marsh. It was

a bottomless place. Mingling of fresh
and salt water, our ankles steeped
in tidal brine as we combed the sands
                    for treasure.

Now ebb tide, the black mud salted
with egrets, last light glinting off her
gray-blond hair as she searches for clams.
She takes my hand, polishes its ooze,
points to the great blue heron wading
from the edge of the marsh. A gust of wind,
late summer. He lifts over the waves,
            spreads his wide wings east.

To be in any form, what is that?
(Round and round we go, all of us, and ever come back thither,)
If nothing lay more develop'd the quahaug in its callous shell were enough.

—Walt Whitman

GEOMETRY

In every place there is arrangement. Order of
             parked cars, sunrises,
the particular poppies lazing
under a south facing window, all
             the sides of any house in various weathers.

There is a street, just so, and the desert
             empty of streets. There is a lake, an ocean,
a boat knocking against the dock, a thousand
             lobster toggles gathered
        on the shore, expectant.

When I was eight, the coast of Maine, endless
uninhabited islands, the rocky inlets and pines, rowing
        the leaky dinghy, my hands
stained with blueberries. How one moon

with a singular brightness will shine
the script of many fields: the brittle stalks and furrows,
             the snow silting white and black,
plots, plows, races, all redolent crops and bodies
        driven by dreams. Dreams:

in a southern dawn, a man is watching television. A storm
             reminds him of the Weather Channel, and he is
one breath, numerous states, the distance
             of water and mind. Now a spark outside

is a place in the past: a dock, a girl, some loons
and scattered lightning. Cries. Laughter. Another dawn.
             Live remote, he listens but cannot go back.

Now the room alights, there is light and what is seen by it.

There is your face, not here, but remembered, close,
        your body's singular brightness.
             There is a ways
and means to gathering, memory
and its suit of hooks.

And when this hunger is not yet a wound,
when the blade of delight has not yet cut, we are,
            are we not, wishing, the open window, and there
                        someone familiar
coming through the grass.

            Islands. Row boats. The riven bark of a certain tree.
The arc of a rope swing lazing over a creek in mid-summer.
                        I paint a picture,
it comes back to me. I use the first person
            and am familiar. Arrangement is one thing here
            a child swinging through grass.

Walking up the stairs this morning, having forgotten…
            Walking up the stairs like the real gesture
of returning, it is the keys
I'm after, any house, any car, what is gathering there.

                        Perhaps the time
it takes to know someone, to begin the voice
            that speaks between two people, the third person
                        created out of air and more than
desire. Hope's triangulation. A painting hangs

            in a hallway, the perfect brushstroke of wish
and wish. It is the face of Vermeer's girl at dawn, a vase of peonies,
            riotous pink fragrance, and oranges half-spilled
                        onto the living-room floor. The man

admires the acts of the body, the way this wish
            has survived. That the body of light is separate
and inconsolable, that he has died
                        for trying.

Now the man says *to praise* and is not there, his voice
a ghost, lyrical enough, his gaze at the TV glass and anyone
            coming through the grass

or just coming, a brief flex of the hand, open and shut.

My ancestors offer *pass, go through, cut off*
                              the mind road. But it is not
that simple, parables are parabolic. I am rowing, painting,
        thinking the spark in or out. The ghost says *pass,*

        go through, the man rises up to the light,
                      and the table of oranges leans
into the room. Mind is water,

a particle, a wave. Arrangement is just one thing.
        And like a finger pointing, there is
                your face, a leaky boat,
the moon of tomorrow wanting. There is a script

I would write of deserts and parked cars. Island dreams,
        the gathering snow, a thousand poppies
                                        bursting
                under the window, insatiable.

Resembling Her

A fable about a dreamer who has grown so as to outlast the first vase of her body. No, a cautionary tale about an artist, an artist from Baltimore, who, in her flaming hair, wishes the next shape into a sculpture resembling bees or flight or barbed wire. She sweeps the cedar boards of her studio and is unusually sad. Something about a lover who details the fragrant city, the seashore where they ate blue crabs, crusty bread, enormous bowls of gooseberries. Her broom moves like a slow clock, and she remembers Africa, the griot in Senegal telling his circular stories, the fire and rancid tea, the chaff in a gust against the cerulean sky, and the man who seduced her, his violent sweat, his wives in the next room clicking and chattering. A feeling she knows with her fingertips, delicate brushing which becomes the will of a form. Flame, host, conversation. *In clay lives a measure, menagerie, a man and a woman burning the rooms that they live in...*

SUCCESS

Of course it's an old paradox, and that's how we earn it,
one step in the right direction countervailed by lust.

I go to a lecture on Keats. He is still dying in the eye of
his twenty-fifth birthday. Then a friend arrives from out of state

to say she is no longer alone, that success in her case is a nine-
month sentence, a line that is moving to swell out her frame

into an unwanted name. Or a student, not quite a friend, who years ago
in the shadow of a great loss tattooed her skin with a ribbon

of witness, who now stands in my office on the brink of another
friendship to tell me she is positive, how things line up

with other things, the meticulous darkness of blood. Lust is one word
for devouring, success an evening of the score. Warranty,

return address, what is ever covered except rest? All disclosures are
beautiful. All disclosures add up points with beautiful futility.

The trail of waking's a complicated dream. *Half in love with easeful
Death,* this wage of games or speeches, a player leans into

another as a way to get home, and going, there's little to add up
in the heart of the heart of the smoking bar. Now it is August,

now it's a year, and I'm trying to open the good words to the morning
air to somehow calm the need for elsewhere. It's lunch, bleak urges

of a cheap motel. Plots, bills, sweepstakes. A jade plant to Virginia
for a lover who has lost someone. People desire every day

for the wrong reasons. Are the best wishes possible for more wishes,
the genie's trick, time in a bottle, that hunger rises senseless? Like or as,

sadness and return, this travel of souls picks up a body of words.
You attaches to I, two voices illustrate where once there were

none. Briefly there's a pattern to all that's undone. Any system's incorrigible. It clarifies by burns. To leave things is to flourish.

Our hour of sweat is entrance to the dance. The black car purrs. The rock star finds an eye. A waking song in stages. "One, two,"

it all adds up to takes. Flesh, our one possession, the heart is its own redress. Cell of cells, a flower, our passion blooms regardless.

To a Child Arrived Too Soon

Winter still, the storm down, the silk lip
of the moon tasting the ice-white walnuts:
a thought (not even a memory

now) of a face in a poem that reminds me,
write a poem. Sad remonstrance. That we are
all preamble once, and sometimes

emerge like a moon which covets sky
too slow. You have never been
though you were the scar that held us.

Risings pared thin, the push and pull
of the bed and the pen, even now a grace
and violence. The heart breaks to know this,

that the selfish bone inside me could not break,
and so now you grow, a silence. I earned you
through sleep or sleeplessness.

Or I have made you like a bed ten thousand times,
a sheet of skin I peel back to see my clutched frame:
seul self, the smallest brain in the walnut

we all resemble. What chance it was
or worse, you would swim down the body
of love so soon. A poem is good faith

become a bad design. Like a crocus caught
in the net of a freezing rain, we write or rise
too late, too soon, goodbyes before beginnings.

Leaf or Tongue

There is a tree that begins each day with its own rustling. Back and forth, back and forth, it begs to be personified. Yet it keeps on at the very ordinary pace that it keeps on. Hopeful, perhaps, or it is nice to think so, and in the spring it will throw up its green flame like a diva's voice that sings in another language. Another language. What were we about to say? Mouths open, each time, is this our voice? My daughter cries. The son I do not have asks for instruction; how to glue the bumper on the model van, or, do skeletons go to heaven just like angels? You wait, the silent second person, beginning, beginning…and the tree moves. Now its leaves are out. Now you say, wait, stop, look in my perfect green eyes. We can go on like this with our reading and hand-building. The person changes each day, but the wish is the same. The tree knows this with its perfect history of veins and possible branchings, and no matter how hard I think my way into color I will never turn red or gold, never learn to drop myself helically from the highest branch. In the morning we go our separate ways. The wind begins to say. Speaking for the other or not at all.

After Raking Leaves

The rake stands still against the house,
tines of shadow and streetlight limned
like a moon worked through the thresh of maple
as it climbs, and I am tired now. By turns
of a year in a yard *blah blah*, the middle
of a sweat that's full of fear. Piles surround
the sprinkler heads, the desiccated rose,
rhododendron. Smoke rears, it feathers
from the neighbors and so strange,
his chimney's resinous tinge
descriptive, an urgency I do not understand.
The light's held tight in the hedges,
on plastic slides, fallen trikes and skunks,
is filling a yard not my own.
I'm raking other's lawns and then
their poems, my ache-through window pane
drawn off from barrels of mulch and thorns,
more diapers, pizza boxes, cartons and cans,
what form of dream that's made unclear
aware of the great harvest. To bear
another and love despite. What death
in fear, this routine rumble of bins,
And, I admit, what life—a sister, now
her son, his just sprung pink
and powder smell a lull
in the carnival coming-and-going.
There's a bond between rake
and grass, as in a mother in a son,
the pull through tangle of stones and stems
that bear a hurt, a stooping. Teeth gnash
in picking. A man is but a walking
comb strutting across the lawn. To hear
his drag down still—that four
then two then three long-pointed knave
who pokes the ground—it's comical.
Happiness has no terminus or tools.
My Frost believes he's spanned a secret ladder
but to where? This poem goes on for years
plumbing the depths of the parking lot, riddle
of strip malls from farms. Heaven's a faith,

in human shàpe. The climb out of the self
is sonorous but cold. Mother,
a garage door opens down the street,
semiotique. It swings a hinge
to sky and grass. And still I rake to keep
the sound. And still my sleep returns.

STORY

... vignette vindaloo, *res* roulette, try one two three
endless possibility chainsawing the inexhaustible
dark wood of memory—the scream,
the teeth biting the neck

at a party near a pool when
the keg was dry, our Hero was flush
and jealousy, rich with others,
had arrived

in a bronze Monte Carlo...
and later, *so it goes*, a fleeting scene
with a waitress named Charlotte
from Coeur d'Alaine, too much drink

too *conflict* too fast, the after seduction
of blur and regret, some new neck
pulled from the toilet despairing
of a father who had...

and earlier, *when, when...*
when the last boat of an old world
had arrived from Cape Valiant Wherever,
and the cardboard and twine

of possession stepped off carrying
cardboard and twine...and made it, somehow,
by pluck and determination, engineering out
of the North Woods, an old saw

about cutting through logs cleanly enough
to build houses, wan light, Valhalla,
dreams... This goes on for fifty
chapters, is a drama of infinite jest

as they say, copywriting the absurdity
of individuation, or the commonly held
belief that we grow into the universal
as we read. Everything's reading,

and the trees excellent text
to learn our alienation. *Double entry.* Imagination's
reciprocity, either learning or being bored,
and the world's bored from it. For instance

some author, let's say you, and his
prophetic destiny to *tell it like it is*
and not be heard, like right now that couple
yawning, these Portuguese fishermen

dancing round a salty fire, *dramatic necessity*
full of sherry and kale, jigs
on the love of women
not gone—they

could give a shit, and do
in the large scheme of things, remember.
Scheme. Stratagem. Plan
to cease all plotting, the paradox

of fictive endings which might still be
another beginning, stories to live by ceaselessly, time
hungry telling into the dark,
and the paragraphs

in our voices forming shapes
around the beautifully random—
figures, inevitably of speech we are
up in prayer, down at the drive-in, *yes*

Mary Beth in the rumble seat, sisters
in the rumble seat, aunts, uncles, *complication*—
enemies with their knives and conceits
of exploding popcorn, the thin line

of inflection linking a star
to an ear, to the ebbing harbor slough
where possum burrow, and raccoon paw through garbage
in the moonlit shadows…

where the mighty jaws of a shark
might possibly eat someone, mercy
near an island, high summer, the screams of bathers
rising out of the surf, and the Sheriff,

who knew the story, *who told everyone*
and now must tell it again, the way it will be,
archetypal movie, the always driving
driving home, the honeyed sound of *Earth*

Wind, and Fire, "Groove Thing,"
and where it will take you, this time me
with a girl who's becoming a story
of a woman, something

right and true in the telling…
that I am implicated in such a way as to
forestall ironic proclivities, overcome willful projections.
That the narrative dimension is inherent

in the human condition, spells out
the manifold twining of animals,
corpuscles, economics, shoe size, flowers, etc.
may they all be present, and You

who will rise again for no reason other
than curiosity, other than love, *periodic*
of the next beginning, one shining island
to be linked and cut, linked and cut,

linked and cut . .

THE ART OF NAVIGATION

Soul itch, hour wife, heaven jar,
        I want to write you a love poem, exquisite braid
of wind in the wheat,
        bells victorious

    tolling the morning light
like Latin poets do. Or dusk's bird swarm, feeling of
        scatter and bank, the sodium sky
        held up *held up*
by the elm's last limb, dying filigree

is everywhere next to you. But irony,
        my will is weak, I grow strong in shallow harbors,
cast images from whiskey and cheese cloth,
    rake sand and the dog evenly. Such armatures

        of sadness
and whim, asymptotic necessity
to be close, to run. Where is the joy in longing? The eternal lyre
        does, so let's be straight: all fruition

is a fiction, a frisson of stars, a place in the deep's
    mother panes which does not flash.

        Then O spring says
in the mouth of the lily,
        and there are geese
in the sky pond, ants in my beard, a *bodying forth*
    of redbud, jams and shoulders, and wind

    damnable wind, repeating gesture of
coming down from the mountains palming everything...

The revolution stutters to a halt. Your eyes, rocked fissures
        yielding heat like a mineral squint,
    do nothing for me. They do not write
or rise or turn from their bony chair, and what I

would give you requires work, fool's coordinates, a sex-
         tant's risk, more sleeping next to
complex ideas, contiguous

but afraid. Little witch, I dull and keen, I want to write you
         a love poem. But anomie, another night, how to walk under
                           the water, how
              to make failures shine?

TRAVELING PAPERS

Creak of this or that. Furniture. Ankle joint. Joists in the floors where mice. The filter of water from an upstairs place. That you climb it again these years. "We had a catamaran that hummed in its front yard rest." Vined with ivy. Two hulls are an answer. Pas and Mas. A point where the light sweeps to sea and pulls the flotsam back. What to shop for what sustains? Driftwood burl, salmon lure, beach glass blown into a '20s blue? "They don't make that no more" except coasters, metaphors, traveling papers. Ambergris is a word. "With rose-petaled scents will we all be revived." A recherché try. A subdivision of voices still seeking whales. "Why do men leave and women stay?" Why do we say it this way? To my friends all a'snug in their harbors. To the innumerable reels of movie waves. To galleon dreams. Romantic projection. Creak of this or that. A type of sounding that carries faces, the writer's child unborn. "Sir Francis was vaguely and the light spirals my body." The small sea of the swimming pool a Master reply. Marco. Polo. Once the search is in your ears as once a drug suggested Grail you leave. Is a misty seen from a fuzzy sought. Suburban elk with their white asses in the sky vanishing. Home. A spit of land that slid. How to be described? Gray day. Sails. It was always. Then sometimes. Filmy the way of salt. Soft. And the big yellow jackets, moldy rubber boots. Of course in the telling it slides. That you climb it again not a stair as the scenery continually. Why do we say "take care?" It takes regardless. Restless. And the voices are added to pictures. "We had a boat with two hulls. It skimmed and skimmed in the harbor past ducks and milk jug moorings." Lasting's a word with no sense. That it sings.

Although the principles of piloting are simple, they are nevertheless extremely complex. A student of piloting comes to learn the methods of locating position by writ of soundings and objects, lighthouses, beacons, stars. He learns, thereby, a means of making charts, labeling and recording them, interpreting their movements as the relative motion of land-scapes and oars. Moreover the same procedures for locating position by celestial travel obtain as a matter of soul,

he who walks with his house on his head is heaven

WORLD SAID

Come home now and you shall hear it, the root
        vowel caught on the reeds
your dailiness, plosive rushes
                your just said sum and sunder. Say

light and dark apple of seed, the scuttered can
              relaxing, say print of a moth wing
      every gray
an interval pressed into

        like a science a synapse opening the mouth
its cupping going round into living tissue

these shapes and silences moving in the latticed world
      inarticulate

sighs of plumbing, the constant
          boulevard thrum, stitch of wind
     of the refrigerator, patient

fingers of rain on a metal roof
      and the gnash of ginkos loosing their fans
at the yellow edge of fall.

At night Iconology tells you
         the lone motorcycle zippering up
    the hillside, a curve
and a place
       in memory's ear
the actual cough lining up with every cough

is measure
is wanting flesh on air.

The palm is rising out of its clutch, speech
     a ripple the ear is prone to

listen, slow rasp, your life in its miter box
                    grooves
against sleep, a breathing shroud and
                    blowing, death rattle of something

one arm finding music against skin
or the sudden waterglass.

In this the dread opens up, a wail
          the trombone blows, its brass nose you stand up in
                              braying
            self's bright song

like day sounds, their punctual tap on routine
          cash register tickering at the dinner glass

fumbling spindles of ignition, waiting
                              the catch, the ear
                    always waiting.

To trace out the list the long way home
          phonemes beck
and call
          like the telephone
                    like the blue jays' machine gun caw looping
                              over the cats
hidden
in the grass, and the oak ball's random thump
                    on the deck, all this and the front door

slammed with the urgency of late, something to every
listening
          giving you away. Words are

giving out ways, are
giving you dark olives in a season's mouth, arrival
                    at what hums
your lips
          the first purse repeated

                              tattered, your

cry's white emblem.

Say come home now and you shall hear it, the way

              sounds enter breath, all
you cannot be, the way

sounds haunt as ash, like a tail
                                        two steps
                      behind the jet, a

noiseless shell of blue, ear
                                   as it was
              our trebled spur riffling the thick of it.

MY BRUEGHEL

Some of us have wiles, Porsches, saxophones,
the mower lawned and craving mums,

and many days, fires, no fire, frost and habitation
and the calendars click into place. Luck!

What have you. Lottery of nights and sweats,
Motown, oiled brushes, variety in oranges

and sheens. Think of albumen fields, blackest
elders, and here my Brueghel loves me. Many

are the one to preserve emblematic. I serve
voices and hives with a mind full of honey

and rest awhile, stay stammer shadow. The roar
of the North and the sough of the pipes, how Faith

goes out for drinks, cigarettes, finds Still Life
to slake the coffers. Psychic landscape, it's a need

and here my Brueghel. I dream winter scenes, folklore
imperative, der poof! and in High German. Whatever signs

to the receptive. It's dog and the smell of dog,
the blind lady palming a bowl of wheat, ever anon

suggestive, avatars branched in the snow. To be set off
[magic bracket], to continue nonetheless. The star falls

in the middle of the dance floor, miraculous ribbons
of magnesium. She's a messenger for incompletion

—dash, sixth sense of the wishing. The well goes on
with its waters, compounding the bedrock

which is a source also. Like turnstiles, house calls,
May Queen inversions, a wolf at the door and the art

full of rooms. Mr. Corpse, are you listening? Living's
a pigment to peel. All of us Brueghels, pirates, veneers.

E IS FOR EVIDENCE

*"An idea, a relationship, can go extinct, just like
an animal or a plant."*
—Bill McKibben

Fire is hunger, imperative, heat. A lighthouse,
corrosion, the natural agency of a ruddy glow.
Of element, this fyre is named the elixir vitae.
To give out the body, to set the cask, to state
all our brilliant combustions. As virtues go,

Water is found more widely, the liquid of
composure. Contrasted with wine, *the drinke
of plantes and animals.* Rivers, oceans, tears,
rain, in phrases, navigation. Journey relating
to use. Of runnel and spit, something to birth,
Halfe of what weare made of, halfe of what

we dreame. Air is countenance, the look of man
or woman. That which rises, impalpable essence
of Mind. Connective scale, a gas. Bad attitude or
music, exposing oneself to God. His chambered shell,
Her breathing, *this fine right currency of wind.*

Earth is forms, *to plough the goode roade,*
committing our hands to rest. Our present sentence
between Heaven and Hell. A world resembling
habitable space. Chiefly all our origins.
Almond, currant, divination, salt, *Dar'st thou,
thou little better thing than earth.*

(Re)Cento

Perhaps in the circumference of story, tour knowledge to purify self,
a reckoning of dimensions more historical by drift (say field trip,

resistance, creak of this or that). You wake to feel the weight
like atom's blessing. In every arrangement a place, word's roving

combustion and the scenery continually. Gender is a muscle
that moves from room to room, a measure of desire, yes?, axis

that wishes obtain. *Oh Continental, durable lies*, resemble her
who was missing. My book of hunger the paradox of blood,

it blooms regardless, restless, and the voices are added to pictures.
Come home now I cast on shivered skin. (Here's a boy on a Big Wheel

in the Fundi's slack singing a song from America.) Always the where
you are ahead thirty yards in the snow like a spectral hand. Soul itch,

how to be described? Consumptive. Arboreal. Exactly the color of cold.
That the selfish bone inside me could not break. There is something

suspicious in the poetics of endless return. And later, when I'm just
eating eggs, something like pleasure, dark olives in a season's mouth.

Mother, the intricate weave of the Green Man is an exile that no thing
describes. He throws up his flame in the marrow, and what will be

my Golden Hind? I drive north in a scudding towards the Neva. Speech
falls out of the sky like a dinner bell. Gray days, sails, it was always

a song, what comes between. These idylls of convenience have intention
and a cause. Seance. Two voices are better if used by love, it's a part

of you already. Grace gives us recurrence, a resinous sun. If Father
is my shell game, I will make him run and run. *Vida Vagabundo,* forgive

this act of refraction. My model's assembled by suit of hooks. Never-
theless, what do we forget in books? Enter widely. Practice. Be. Trust

is the goode roade is earth (light and dark apple of seed). Look out the
window, child. You rasp and rise from the coral lips and I am tired now.

TONGUE RUTH

—for Paul Celan

No blessing but muscle
           no reach but stain
no fire but gender or blood. The mouth swells
to contain your voice, the wars
        the stones
       the marrow that reaves out the fields.

Beggars of the tribe go archaic
       rive or down the last, down
and the coldest socket cannot hold me, the ashen
    taste. I break

    off into the smoke light of distances
the enormous Pleiadesian night which is
       beginning to show its haunches.

        Listen
sever and fuse, the code
and I am undone in the blue laddering
the form
and the first eye which stays the air.

Seek me, ask for the blessing, rise up
       for what cannot touch you
         make cord
in the bitter sibilance
burning speech.

The cobs of my story, bones and whistle
thorn which is a bird in the barest sky
       wind which is
a guttural thing
     tuning the stems
dust music.

     To have held your parts, to harrow
the broken letters and tongue
       let down your net.

Once more
I have hidden from you, the defeated, the essential
anatomy. Pocket

and spare
and I will press my hand into you. Indelible
glow
take my name

Then Yetsirah

*"He is a Jew," said Reb Talba. "He is leaning
against a wall, watching the clouds go by."*
                                    —Edmond Jabès

1

In our name's begotten stillness what is first?
          A face,
                the idea of a face, shining
out of the trench of darkness
                a long time

                or the strange garment of journey
worn to thin, the red stitches
                of place,
each body a house, each letter a center
                held against the fretwork of stars,
                                white eyes.

What is last?

*He who is willing to work gives birth
          to his own father.*

2

A child moves out against absence, pushes with his tongue
          against the world.

"Blond boy, what will you write with? How will you know
          your name?"

3

Above the brisket, poised with a knife in mid-stroke
it struck you, this work was as close to religion
        as you came. Catering. Making knishes. Washing
in the back room as Isaac's dream was dancing
        across the parquet of Bethel in a taffeta gown.
It was a job. Continental. And you would burn out
        the clutch of the delivery van, dropping gears
like crumbs all the way from Temple. You were close,
        "in the blood," found the afikomen once.
But the words, the music? Muffled horahs,
        Chagall's lost angels, the scrape of heavy plates.

4

The idea of Number. Of one becoming many.
        Of genitive and magnitude, the terrible august running
                of scale and cell.

                    I and Thou cannot be split.

5

Through the wind I watched him, trimming
        the sea from the sails, a father born
from water, from the salting veil of scars.
        From murmuring pines, a field of shoes,
We are two coasts, one fog, a loss
        to lust and hunger. Like father

like son. Heading up to find a shore. To run
        downwind and tack, to let the jib lines whirl
into a name. I watched him thread the bow
        into the harbor, his stitching hand that held
the night together. Apart or a part? To find that slip
        again, to follow the water stairs down.

6

Yetsirah   *Creation*

Seek the vine of fathers. Peel the skin from a name.

Yetser *means 'form,' 'frame,' 'purpose' and with reference to the mind, 'imagination,'*
or 'device.' The problem of good and evil arises only when there is imagination.

Talmudic tradition refuses to identify the evil yetser *with the body and the good* yetser
with the soul. Such body/soul dichotomies are rejected. The distinction between good and
evil is a moral choice, not the physical property of Being.

7

As a child in Philadelphia my father threw pennies under the streetcars at
Rittenhouse Square. On his way to shul, bright boy of thirteen dragging his
blue and white tallis through the rainy streets. My version drones like fitful
sleep. Out of work. Jesus mutters from the clock radio, "who will be
saved... who is gone?" He is the Lord's Prayer in my pocket when I am thir-
teen. A penny rolled into blessing. He is a joke from my grandfather singed
in the copper mill.

8

Adonai ask Esau, where does a man go?
Wandering is a number. The world itself is wordless.

9

A journey, mine or yours, just beginning,
            the blue light they speak of as my eyes,
my eyes in the back of my grandfather's head.

His head at the beginning, breaching the first air,
            his Mother emerging, the same blood,
the same hay of a Bessarabian barn, the pale light

on the other side of birth. How wide the sea is.
            How many? How slow and hungry
Death dreidling our blue boat.

10

The villagers called him Moshe the Beadle, as though he had never had a surname in his life. He was a man of all work at a Hasidic synagogue. The Jews of Sighet—that little town in Transylvania where I spent my childhood—were very fond of him. He was very poor and lived humbly. Generally my fellow townspeople, though they would help the poor, were not particularly fond of them. Moshe the Beadle was the exception. Nobody ever felt embarrassed by him. Nobody ever felt encumbered by his presence. He was a past master in the art of making himself insignificant, of seeming invisible.

11

To write the world that is wordless.
                        To make visible the many. To find the distant
presence in my weak story. *Thou* are present,
                  and *I* am a past,
            and *we* are all passed through.

12

In a white-screened office of swivel chairs, lab coats, dictaphones and a skeleton named Bruce, I would come to spend lunch with my Father. Barbecue day, turkey legs as big as my thigh, the golden skin and sauce. Papa, wearing green surgical scrubs. The steam and fluorescent air. I'd sit on his lap while he read X-Rays. An arm, chest series, head injury from a motor-cycle accident.

"... Son, don't ride a motorbike, your head is a fragile egg."

Bruce was mounted on swivel wheels, and after lunch we'd slide him back and forth until Papa began to sing "Edelweiss" and waltz him around the room. That was how my mother often found us, glowing in the white-screened luminescence. She'd stand in the doorway smiling, the sports page for my father, a can of iced tea. Bruce would glide off into the corner, and I'd sit on the speckled linoleum, humming "Edelweiss," watching them dance around the room.

13

Maimonides   Yehudah Halvi   Bahya Ibn Pakuda

The Law of the Father is history, is becoming, the ethical robe.

The Law of the Body is blood, dark liquids clotted in the shawl of light.

14

Black and white, the kitchen floor. Squares of home
cut by toys and trucks. Or Mom's green pumps, cat glasses,
bouffant, cooking smells and highballs. Or homemade beer,

now bell-bottoms, Pop's leisure suits, platform shoes, over there
his sideburns. Affairs. The denim workshirts Mom stitched
with suns and birds. Our initials. Wearing them too thin.

Or a father and son on a Schwinn 3-Speed,
new to California, mowing down magnolia leaves
in the first scuttle of fall. Our neighborhood
one place, happy glow of the farthest shore.
You asked me to go to Temple
                  and would I like to learn Hebrew.

echad   shtayim   shalosh   arba   chamesh   shesh

15

Indelible, their forearms, shining in the eastern light.

          Skin is a gown of infinite sadness.

eins   zwei   drei   vier   fünf   sechs

16

alphabets and numbers
           in the undivided air
divided

begin the march
of faith   naming
           the dark cloud
cloud

Aleph said Emeth
           turn Life and Death to dust
in His dry mouth
                         the taste
becoming
           the speech of Good
           and Evil

the first person speaking
           for *I*

17

Blond boy was restless, the sign in his mouth,
the mystic slip of paper. To have written a story
           of swimming and sweating. Of the wheel in the sea
passing under him, and the wave's white stitch toward shore.
           On the slip he reads his wander, how he's lost
to the wind of what he'll become, the fabric from
           the book, the book of lust and hunger.

18

Papa, forgive me for saying. For naming
        the less

that I am. A son of dispersion,
        a lack

of tongues, there's blood in my eye again.

    Yetsirah

To work, to fall and then work. To make a use
of love. Theft is the mind which imagines it.

one   two   *chai*

        "How will you know My Name?"

Tell me again, Dark Father, re-
        vise, remind…

A world is placed in me (I am placed in the world)

    and shatters

NOTES

To wonder the settle of what becomes, dead reckoning, I guess. A burden in the plumb line, but a singing joy too, a faith in voices, I/ye. *Let us thinke that our Lord God kepeth a reckoning of all the days of our calamitie* (Daus, 1573). And other debts:

"California Dreaming" for the Tong, scattered brothers

"Russian Pictures" for my sister Lisa

"Leaf or Tongue" for Sweet T, mud honey

"Resembling Her," for Martha, Madame Hazard

"The Art of Navigation," for Lizzie

And to books specifically, lines and phrases in the italicized passages on the following pages:

13   "Further Aridity" *you just have to dig for wood and water,* Horace Greeley

37   "Two Waters, respectively: *distance is not a safety net but a zone of tension,* Theodor Adorno, <u>Minima Moralia</u>; the quoted (and not italicized) passage in Ohlone Singing, from <u>The Ohlone Way</u>, by Malcolm Margolin.

53   "Success," *Half in Love with Easeful Death,* Keats' "Ode to a Nightingale."

71   "E is for Evidence" *This Fire is named the Elixir Vitae,* E. Baker, <u>The Jewel of Health</u>; *Dar'st thou, thou little better thing than earth,* Shakespeare, <u>Richard III.</u>

75   "Then Yetsirah," respectively: Kierkegaard, <u>Fear and Trembling</u>; Eric Fromm, <u>You Shall Be as Gods</u>; Elie Wiesel, <u>Night</u>

And to books and passages (sometimes freely) adapted in the Section Headings:

I.   D.J. Jacks, <u>Naval Studies III: Ship's Body</u>

II.   Elizabeth Bishop, "Questions of Travel," <u>Geography</u>.

III.   James Joyce, <u>Ulysses</u>.

IV.   Walt Whitman, "Song of Myself," <u>Leaves of Grass</u>.

V.   Lyman Kells, Willis Kern & James Bland, <u>Piloting and Maneuvering of Ships</u>; and *he who walks with his house on his head is heaven,* Algonquin proverb

And to books (and folks) generally:

"Field Trip" is inspired, in part, by Jim Jarmusch's movie <u>Dead Man.</u>

"For Those Who Would Drown Him" owes inspiration and idiolect from respectively: <u>The Journals of Herman Melville</u>, <u>Collected Letters of Hart Crane,</u> and <u>Charles Olson and Robert Creeley: The Complete Correspondence</u>.

"Geometry" is in conversation with Robert Hass' two "Spring Drawing" poems from <u>Human Wishes</u>.

"After Raking Leaves" quite directly riffs on Robert Frost's famous poem "After Apple-Picking"

Sacrificial zincs are anti-fouling devices attached to the bottom of metal-hulled boats to prevent corrosion. Their development in the post-wooden ship era represents one of the more ingenious solutions to the ravaging effects of sea water. They work by polarity, attracting the positive ionization of salt water, and thereby saving the less polarized sections of the metal hull. They are available in any marine supply store and come in a variety of sizes and configurations.

Yetsirah is an English transliteration for the Hebrew: creation; *yetser* is an English transliteration of the Hebrew: imagination. Structured on Kabbalist numerology, there are 18 sections to the poem; 18, *chai,* among other things, is an English transliteration for the Hebrew: life.

About the Author

Matthew Cooperman's *Surge* was selected as the winner of the 1999 Wick Chapbook Series and was published by Kent State University Press. His poems appear in *Chicago Review, Denver Quarterly, Black Warrior Review, Quarterly West* and elsewhere. *A Sacrificial Zinc* was selected for the Lena-Miles Wever Todd Poetry Series by Susan Ludvigson.

About the Lena-Miles Wever Todd Poetry Series

The editors and directors of the Lena-Miles Wever Todd Poetry Series select one book of poems for publication by Pleiades Press each year. All selection are made blind to authorship in an open competition for which any American poet is eligible. Past winners include Al Maginnes for *The Light in Our Houses* (Betty Adcock, final judge) and Kevin Prufer for *Strange Wood* (Andrea Hollander Budy, final judge).